Moving Day Surprise

written by Tina Stolberg
illustrated by Nicole Tadgell

Bebop Books
An imprint of LEE & LOW BOOKS Inc.

My family lives in an apartment.
This is my room.
This is my fish, Flipper.

Our apartment is big enough for three people and one fish.

But now we have a new baby.
"Our apartment is too small," says Papa.
"We need more room," says Mama.

On Sunday Mama and Papa
go to find a bigger apartment.
Grandma stays with me
and the baby.

I tell Grandma my secret.
"Flipper likes his friends and his school," I say.
"He will miss them if he moves away."

"I didn't know Flipper went to school," says Grandma. Grandma tickles me and I feel better.

Mama and Papa come home.
They look happy.
They have found a bigger apartment.
"We move next weekend," says Mama.
I am sad.
Flipper is sad too.

On Friday night Mama gives me
a box to pack my toys.
I put everything in the box
except Flipper.

On Saturday we are all packed.
"We are ready to go," says Papa.

We get on the elevator.
We do not go down.
We go up to the sixth floor.

10
11
12
7
8
9
4
5
6
3

"Who lives on six?" I ask.
"We do now," says Papa.
"This apartment is big enough for
four people and one fish," says Mama.

Flipper is happy.
I am happy too.